Presented to _____

by _____

on _____

the growing reader

Book of Prayers

written by
Joy MacKenzie

illustrated by
Jill Newton

TYNDALE KiDS

Tyndale House Publishers, Inc.
Wheaton, Illinois

Edited by Betty Free Swanberg
Designed by Julie Chen

Published in association with the literary agency of Ann Spangler & Associates, 1420 Pontiac Road Southeast, Grand Rapids, MI 49506.

Library of Congress Cataloging-in-Publication Data

MacKenzie, Joy.
    The growing reader book of prayers / Joy MacKenzie ; illustrated by Jill Newton.
        p. cm.
    Includes index.
    Summary: A collection of prayers of worship and praise, thanksgiving, celebration, confession, intercession, and petition that address concerns of children introduce phonetic sounds from A to Z.
    ISBN: 0-8423-8479-0 (hc : alk. paper)
    1. Christian children—Prayer-books and devotions—English.   2. Reading—Phonetic method—Juvenile literature. [1. Prayer books and devotions.   2. Readers.   3. English language—Phonetics.]   I. Newton, Jill, ill.   II. Title.
BV265.M25 2004
242'.82—dc22   2003020696

Printed in Singapore

13   12   11   10   09   08   07   06   05   04
10   9   8   7   6   5   4   3   2   1

Contents

Teaching Your Child to Pray and Read

The Growing Reader Book of Prayers is about discovering why and how we talk to God in ordinary language about real things. Along with its companion, *The Growing Reader Phonics Bible*, it notes and facilitates the phonics approach to reading. However, it does this without distraction from the primary purpose of enriching young children's understanding of the person of God, his care for them, and his availability to them in everyday, anywhere-anytime conversation.

The model prayers of worship and praise, thanksgiving, celebration, confession, intercession, and petition address the fears, anxieties, questions, and concerns of children.

In the context of charming rhymes, rhythms, sounds, and illustrations that captivate the attention of fledgling readers, children will also discover that God talks to us in many ways, often speaking to our hearts inaudibly, but in a manner that is undeniably real. If we are quiet before him, we can understand what he is telling us.

"Don't worry about anything; instead, pray about everything. Tell God what you need, and thank him for all he has done" (Philippians 4:6).

Beginning readers who aren't yet ready to read the prayers themselves *are* ready to listen. In each prayer, they will delight in hearing a *star sound* of our language and seeing it identified in color. Slowly and surely the relationship between the squiggly lines on a page and the sounds those squiggles stand for will begin to make sense. Then those wiggly little people will be well on their way to becoming irrevocable readers.

Maturing readers will experience the joy of becoming more and more independent as relationships between sounds and letters leap into focus. This happens as they see the same colored letters repeated again and again in a prayer. They will find these letters in words that are woven together to create enticing rhyme and alliterative language play as they engage in the fun of voraciously attacking and devouring words and ideas on their own.

All growing readers (including those already grown in age) will take delight in these prayers, rich in sound and color, as well as in imaginative illustrations that magnify the prayers' meanings.

My prayer is that boys and girls and their grown-up friends will meet God in these pages so that they will develop a greater appreciation of his care for them and his joy over them. I pray also that they may come to understand that prayer is the privilege of access to God. His purpose is to develop a deep, intimate love relationship with each one of them.

May you find great delight in using this book—morning and evening; alone or together as parent and child, brother and sister, or friends; and in fellowship with others as you celebrate very special occasions.

Joy MacKenzie

Tell It to the Great, Big King

CONVERSATIONS WITH GOD

When you are bothered by hurts and ouches,
And you are tired of grumps and grouches;
Or when you are happy and ready to burst
With joy and laughter, then hurry! The first
Person who loves you and wants to share
Is the one who is always EVERYWHERE.
And he's patiently waiting to hear you say
Whatever you feel as you come to pray.

> *So tell it! Tell it to the great, big King.*
> *You can tell him anything!*
> *Any time and anywhere*
> *Is the time and the place to say your prayer.*

When you have a special secret to tell,
Then whisper to One who will keep it well.
When something you thought could NOT happen
*   DID,*
And you hated it so that you ran and hid,

And you don't have a friend who
   knows how you feel . . .
There's someone who does. He cares—and he's
   REAL!
      So tell it! Tell it to the great, big King.
      You can tell him anything!
      Any time and anywhere
      Is the time and the place to say your prayer.

Do you have a friend who is lonely or sad,
Or afraid or mad about something bad?
Or maybe he's feeling down in the dumps
'Cuz his life is full of bruises and bumps.

Well, you have a God who's ALREADY KNOWING
Exactly how your friend's day is going.
God's always near—he's not far away—
And he's ready to help, both night and day.

So talk about your friend
  to the great, big King.
You can tell him anything!
Any time and anywhere
Is the time and the place to say your prayer.

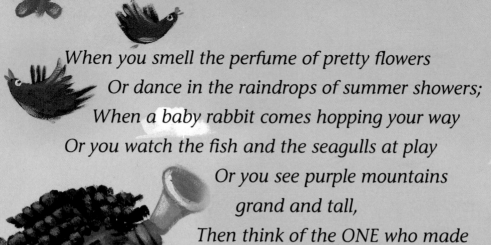

When you smell the perfume of pretty flowers
Or dance in the raindrops of summer showers;
When a baby rabbit comes hopping your way
Or you watch the fish and the seagulls at play
Or you see purple mountains
grand and tall,
Then think of the ONE who made
them ALL
And shout for joy! Strike up the band!
Celebrate God! Give him a hand!
Say, "Thank you! Thank you, my
God and King,
For you have created everything!
And now I'll be quiet—as still as
can be,
So I can hear YOU talking to ME!"

A Prayer for Forgiveness

WHEN I HURT OTHERS AND MAKE GOD SAD

Every time I make a mistake
I say, "Hey, Lamebrain! What will it take
To never EVER do that again?"
I promise myself I'll do better, and then—
Well, perfect I'll never be able to be,
And the only one I can blame is me!
I'm just like Jonah and Joseph's brothers,
And Adam and Eve and all the others.

I want to be good. I try to obey.
And I hate it that I cannot seem to stay
Out of trouble for even a day!
Again and again, I need to pray.
And so I bow my head in shame.
What if God gets tired of hearing my name?

Dear God, I made a mistake today.
And it hurt someone, so I came to say
I'm sorry. Forgive me. I take the blame.
Please hug this person. Here is the name:

Hug ____. [Say the name of the one you hurt.]
Thanks a lot, God! Amen.

In Your Bible

Find the story about a boy who ran away and made his father sad. See how his father forgave him and hugged him. That is how our heavenly Father acts when we are sorry for wrong things we do—mistakes that hurt other people and make God sad. Look for the story in Luke 15:11-32. (If you have *The Growing Reader Phonics Bible*, you'll find it on pages 334–340.)

A Prayer of Praise

BECAUSE I AM LIVING AND BREATHING

Let everything that has breath praise the Lord. Psalm 150:6

If I am breathing, then I guess
I should be praising. Yes! Oh yes!
Like Noah and his family,
And the blind man Jesus made to see;
Like Daniel in the lions' den,
And the sheep that was lost but found again—
I know God hears all of my requests,
And he's the one who loves me best.

O Father God, your name
  I bless.
I praise you that I
  can express

My smallest joy or biggest pout,
And you will always hear me out.
You treat me as a welcome guest
And put my hurts and fears
    to rest.
So in a quiet, gentle voice,
I want to tell you I rejoice
That you have given breath to me.
Yes, I exalt you joyfully!

In Your Bible

Look for a story about two sisters who were sad because their brother had died. They cried out to Jesus, and he gave their brother new life. Oh, were they happy then! You can find the story in John 11:1-45. (If you have *The Growing Reader Phonics Bible,* you'll find it on pages 345–351.)

A Thanksgiving Prayer

TO CELEBRATE GOD'S GIFTS OF GOOD THINGS

A daddy who loves his children
Gives them all things good,
So I am not at all surprised
That you, my heavenly Daddy, would
Want to give to the kids you love
The things that make them glad.
I'm sending this special "thank you,"
And then I'd like to add
A list of the things I enjoy the most—
The things that make me smile.
(I'll find some paper so
I can write
Some others after
a while.)

For sandwiches with melted cheese,
Mashed potatoes and Christmas trees,
Zoos with zebras and birds that fly,
And Grandma's frozen chocolate pie;
For winter snows, and a cozy bed
With mounds of pillows around my head;
My kitten's fuzzy, soft white paws,
The Wizard of Oz and Santa Claus.

For merry-go-rounds that make me dizzy
And puzzles that keep my brain cells busy;

A puppy dog that pulls my clothes
And nuzzles me with his cold, wet nose;
For summer nights with fireflies,
And a baseball mitt that's just my size;
For books and bikes and a tire swing,
And more than I need of everything,
  I THANK YOU, GOD!

In Your Bible
God is the best gift-giver ever! Sometimes he gives things that seem impossible. You can learn about some of those impossible gifts in stories about the prophet Elijah. They are in 1 Kings 17. (If you have *The Growing Reader Phonics Bible,* you will find them on pages 163–171.)

A Morning Prayer

ABOUT MORNINGS

On the first day of creation,
When all the world was new
And everything was perfect,
God was the ONLY "who."
That's when he made the morning.
He said, "Let there be light!"
He spoke into the darkness
To divide the day from night.
But morning is my favorite
   time:
"Surprise!" it says. "I'm
   new!"
So, wide-eyed, I wake
   up and answer,
"Day, how do you do!"

Dear God, I thank you for bright mornings

When everything is quite

Brand-new without mistakes and hurts—

Still safe and sweet and right.

And I just want to tell you

How kind you are—and smart

To give us every single day

A fresh, new start!

In Your Bible

You can read about the very first morning in your Bible. The story is in Genesis 1:1-5. (If you have *The Growing Reader Phonics Bible,* you'll find it on pages 2–7.)

An Evening Prayer

ABOUT WANTING TO BE GOOD

The day is over and night has begun,
And I'm thinking over the things I have done.
I'm not very good at being good,
Nor at doing and saying what I wish
  I would,
For no matter how fine I start out to be,
I end up being the same old me.

"I'll never deny you," said Peter, your friend.
"I'll be by your side to the very end."
Then, before the rooster had done his crowing,
Peter had lied about ever knowing
You, dear Jesus—he sounds just like me,
Though a daring Daniel I'd rather be!

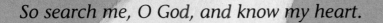

So search me, O God, and know my heart.
  And don't let bad thinking keep
  me apart
  From your Word. Then point
  out my wicked ways
  And be my guide through
  all of my days.

  P.S.
  Did you make nighttime
  so kids like me would
  Have time to catch up on
  being good?

  Great idea! Thanks,
  God!

In Your Bible
Look for the happy story about Daniel, who wasn't
afraid to obey God. You'll find his story in Daniel 6.
(If you have *The Growing Reader Phonics Bible,* you'll
find it on pages 231–237.)

18

A Prayer for Forgiveness

WHEN I FORGET TO TALK TO GOD

It's me again, Lord, and I'm in trouble—
I've hit a bump and burst my bubble.
But first, I must apologize
'Cuz it's been so long since I was wise
Enough to stop in all my rush
And come to you and kneel and hush,
And feel your touch—just be
* your child*
Instead of always running wild.

Oh yes, you know I start to munch
Before I thank you for my lunch.
And often I climb into bed
Forgetting that I haven't said

19

"I love you" and "I care"—Well, duh!
Now how could you believe that, huh?
Well, anyway, my prayer today
Is just to forgive me, please—okay?
And help me dump the stupid stuff
And learn to trust you. That's enough!

P.S.
In case I forget tomorrow to say
How thankful I am, I'll say it today:
For food and love and my friends and such,
I thank you ahead. Thanks VERY MUCH!

In Your Bible

The children of Israel had lots of bumps and troubles when they were walking across the desert. Even after all that God had done for them, they kept forgetting to thank him. Read about that in Exodus 14:21-22 and 16:1–17:7. You will see how God forgives and takes care of his children, even when they forget him. (If you have *The Growing Reader Phonics Bible*, see pages 95–100 and 101–105.)

f

f as in five
gh as in laugh
ph as in alphabet

A Table Prayer

THANKSGIVING FOR GOD'S GIFTS OF FOOD

I like to imagine a photograph
Of a wonderful picnic that makes me laugh.
It's about the boy with five loaves and two fish.
Just the stuff Jesus needed to make a fine dish—
A meal to feed at least five thousand men.
He held it up high to thank God—and then,
He broke up the food into baskets to pass
To all of the people who sat on the grass.
And when they were full, there were twelve
* baskets more*
Of leftover food to take to the poor!

That story is more than we need for proof
That God knows our needs. He doesn't goof!
And even if things get rough and tough,
His beautiful cupboards are full enough

Of wonderful things that he freely gives.
Whether happy or sad, we can laugh 'cuz he lives,
And he loves us and offers us every good thing
From his Father's house. It's the house of the King!

O Father in heaven, we're thankful for
Your gifts of food, which are often far more
Than what we need to make us grow.
We love you for taking care of us so.
Help us to share what you give us so freely
So we can help others. We mean it. Really!

In Your Bible
Look for the story about Jesus feeding thousands of people with just
five loaves and two fish. You can find the story in John 6:1-13.
(If you have *The Growing Reader Phonics Bible,* you'll find it
on pages 314–321.)

A Together Worship Prayer

TO CELEBRATE GOD, WHO IS HOLY

This worship prayer can be done by just one or two people reading all of the parts. Or it can be done as a group or family prayer.

All: *Holy, holy, holy, Lord.*

   Together we sing holy.

Girl: *God of power, God of might,*

Boy: *God of gladness, God of light.*

Girl: *Heaven and earth you fill with glory.*

Boy: *All creation sings your story:*

Girl: *Glittering stars, gigantic trees,*

Boy: *Gargantuan mountains, blue-green seas*

All: *Sing holy, holy, holy, Lord.*

   Together we sing holy.

All: *Holy, holy, holy, Lord.*

   Together we sing holy.

27

Boys: *God of glory, God of love,*
Giver of gifts sent from above.

Girls: *The greatest gift of all—your Son—*
You gave to save us, every one!

All: *For gifts so dear, we gather here,*
Our voices raise in grateful praise.
Holy, holy, holy, Lord.
Together we sing
holy.

In Your Bible

If you look at the book of Psalms, you will find many more prayers that are songs or psalms of worship and praise.

A Together Song

OF WORSHIP AND THANKSGIVING

Psalm 100

Hey everybody!
Think happy! Think joy!
Shout to the Lord—
Every girl, every boy.
Shout hallelujah!
Holler amen!
Do it together.
Now do it again!
Clap for him. Smile for him.
Just do your part.
Laugh for him. Sing to him
With all your heart!

Know this! He is God.

He made us, and we

Did NOT make him.

How amazing to see

That he knows us and loves us.

We are his sheep.

He cares for us when we're

Awake or asleep.

Come to his house

And be at home there.

Praise him and thank him

For inviting you where

You will be loved forever.

O praise him and then

Sing hallelujah!

Hallelujah! Amen!

In Your Bible

God loves it when his children sing to him and talk with him. Psalms are songs and prayers to God. Psalm 100 is a psalm of worship and thanksgiving. Find it in your Bible. (If you have *The Growing Reader Phonics Bible*, you'll find it on pages 210–213.)

A Morning Prayer

ON THINGS TO THINK ABOUT TODAY

Philippians 4:8

A verse in your Word says that what's in my mind—
Each thing I am thinking—that's what I will find
Makes me talk and act the way that I do.
The thoughts I am thinking will tell on me too.

You say to stick tight to the things that are true;
No fooling—no faking—no tall tales will do.
Just think what is honest, respectful, and right,
And push what is wrong and unfair out of sight.

I must try to think what is pure and clean,
Think everything lovely that I've ever seen.

Can't let my mind travel to ugly places
Where frowns steal smiles from happy faces.

So help me today, Lord, to think and to do
Nothing but things that bring great joy to you.
When I'm in a muddle and don't have a clue,
Set my thoughts on things that remind me of you!

In my mind may I treasure all day and all night
What is true and perfect and pure and right—
Only things that are lovely and pleasant to hear,
Just thoughts that delight and invite good cheer.
All things that are beautiful—God, if you please,
Direct all my thoughts every moment toward
these.

In Your Bible
God tells us exactly how to live good, peaceful lives. We can find his directions in the
Bible in both the Old Testament and the New Testament. In the Old Testament, God
gives us a list of rules for happy living. (If you have *The Growing Reader Phonics Bible,*
you can find this story on pages 106–114.) In the New Testament (Philippians 4:8),
you can read directions for good thoughts that lead to good living. God gave Paul
and Timothy these directions to share with their Christian friends.

A Prayer for Others

FOR THE WORLD'S CHILDREN

I love the story about the day
When Jesus did not send the children away,
But gave to each child his caring touch,
Which told them he loved them very much.
And even today, I know it is true
Each child, dear Father, is loved by you.
But some are poor and hungry and cold,
And don't know this love story I have been told.

So I pray, dear Lord, that you will catch
This world full of children, who do not match.
Give them a hug—let them feel your touch
And know that with you, God, nothing such

As nation or riches or skin color matters,
Nor choice of language in which one chatters:
Chinese or Choctaw, Spanish or Dutch;
Red, yellow, black, and white—yes, the whole
  bunch;
Buddhist and Christian, Muslim and Jew;
Each child in the world is a treasure to you.

Please reach out to hug those with horrible fears.
For those who are sad, please wipe away tears;
Put smiles on their cheeks and a laugh in their
    voices.
Give those who are hungry some good, healthy
    choices

Of food to enjoy, and a warm place to keep
Them safe from all harm as they go to sleep.

And God, one more thing. Could I ask in advance
That you touch my heart often and say, "Here's
  your chance
To make a small difference!" Then right away,
For those children you love very much, I will pray.

Each time God reminds me of a child in the
            world who has a special need, I will
            draw a picture and pray.

In Your Bible
You can read about Jesus
and the children in Mark
10:13-16. (If you have *The
Growing Reader Phonics Bible,*
you will find it on pages
341–344.)

A Prayer on a Traveling Day

FOR PEACE AND SAFETY ON THE WAY

The family van is loaded and packed.
Our heavy bags we've stuffed and stacked.
Now we are about to wave good-bye
And be off on vacation! We need your eye
To watch over us, Lord, and keep us alive
From the time we leave until we arrive.

Protect us from all other drivers' mistakes.
Let our driver know when to put on the brakes.
Make all of our travel activities clever—
Creative and fun, so that no one
is ever
Grouchy or grumpy. And
please help us, Lord,
Not to get even a little
bit bored.

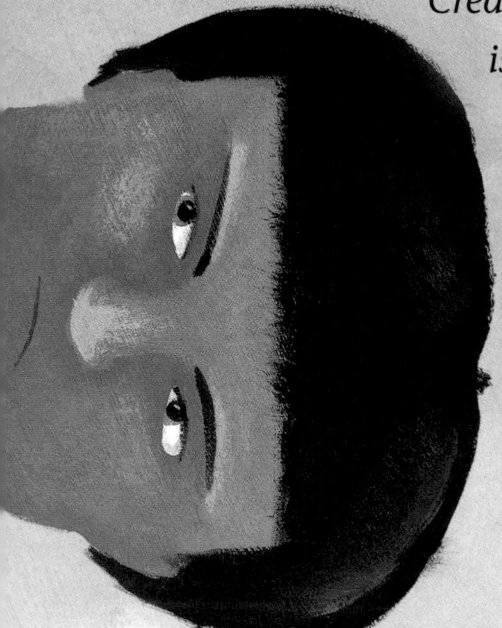

We've got to go easy on
everyone's nerves,
Not lean too far over when
going 'round curves.
We'd love to behave as your Word
tells us to.
May all our adventures be pleasing to you.

P.S.

As we travel, Lord, would you do me a favor?

Get Dad to stop where my favorite flavor

Of ice cream is served—at some real groovy shop,

Where they add lots of sprinkles with whipped
   cream on top.

On the cream they put a very red cherry.

Never would travel be any more merry!

Forgive me if this is a selfish request.

I know you will do, Lord, whatever is best.

In Your Bible
Read about the beginning of the wild and crazy travel adventures of the children of
Israel in Exodus 12–14. See how God watched over them and protected them on
their way from Egypt to their new land. (If you have *The Growing Reader Phonics Bible*,
you can read about the first part of their trip on pages 95–100.)

A Together Worship Prayer

TO CELEBRATE GOD'S CREATION

This celebration prayer may be done by one person reading all the parts;
by two to four people, with one or more of them taking several parts;
or by a group or a family sharing the parts.

Speaker 1: A lot more exciting than a Disney vacation,

More fun than getting a new Dalmatian,

Speaker 2: And far more amazing than magic tricks

Are the things that God made on days five and six!

Speaker 3: He filled his earth with living things
That move with fins and fly with wings!

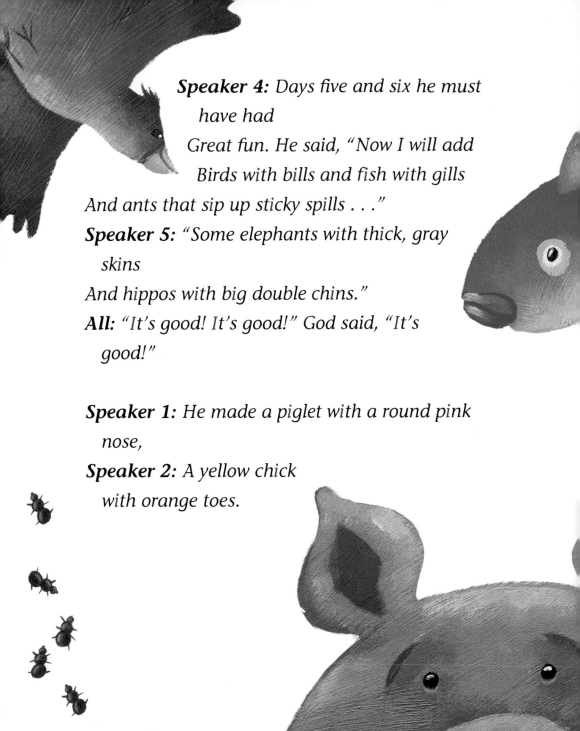

Speaker 4: Days five and six he must
   have had
      Great fun. He said, "Now I will add
         Birds with bills and fish with gills
And ants that sip up sticky spills . . ."
Speaker 5: "Some elephants with thick, gray
   skins
And hippos with big double chins."
All: "It's good! It's good!" God said, "It's
   good!"

Speaker 1: He made a piglet with a round pink
   nose,
Speaker 2: A yellow chick
   with orange toes.

Speaker 3: *Lizards quick that flick their tails,*

Speaker 4: *And slugs with icky, sticky trails.*

Speaker 5: *A ladybug with wings and lots*
Of itsy-bitsy polka dots.

All: *"It's good! It's good!" God said, "It's good!"*

All: *Yes, God, it's good! You said it first!*
It's good! Our hearts and voices burst.
We shout and sing in celebration
Thank you, God, for your creation!

Speaker 1: *It's good!*

Speaker 2: *It's good!*

Speaker 3: *It's good!*

Speaker 4: *It's good!*

Speaker 5: *Yes, it's good!*

All: *It's good, good, GOOD!*

In Your Bible

Look for the story of God's creation of animals in your Bible. It is in Genesis 1:20-25.
(If you have *The Growing Reader Phonics Bible,* you will find this part of the creation
story on pages 12–15.) You can read about all of the days of Creation in Genesis 1–2
(pages 3–18 in *The Growing Reader Phonics Bible*).

A Morning Prayer

ABOUT LISTENING TO MY SHEPHERD

If the Lord is my Shepherd,
Then I am his sheep.
He keeps up with ME
Even when I'm asleep.
He plans to spend time
With me ev'ry day,
But I disappoint him
And wander away.

I don't pay attention
Till I need his help.
But when something bad happens,
I let out a yelp.
My very best friend
He has promised to be,
But I'm not good at hearing
When he speaks to me.

So Jesus, please help me
To hear your kind voice.
And let my mind listen
To the thoughts of your choice.
Then I will wait patiently—
I will prepare
To follow my Shepherd.
This is my prayer.

I'm going to plan
To have times of quiet,
Keep my notebook wide open
And a pencil right by it

To write the ideas
You help me to think.
I'll put them on paper
Quick as a wink!

In Your Bible
The story of the
shepherd who takes
good care of his
sheep, even when
they wander away,
is in Luke 15:1-7.
(If you have *The
Growing Reader
Phonics Bible,*
you will find the
story on pages
329–333.)

A Prayer on a Game Day

FOR SAFETY AND GOOD SPORTSMANSHIP

Today's the big day, and we have got
A game to play. We've done a lot
Of practicing, and we are hot!
Maybe we'll win, or maybe not.
I hope it's okay to ask you, God,
For a little help, though it may seem odd
To request that you stop the other team
From winning, and rob them of their dream.

We'd like to sock 'em—block their plays,
And stop their loyal fans' hoorays,
Then send them sobbing home without
A win. But in my heart, a doubt

Is whispering that my knock-out plot

To whomp and stomp this team is not

Exactly what I should be praying—

Better that I should be saying,

"When the clock says, 'Time to stop,'

We would like to be on top—

Not as a mob of selfish snobs,

But as lots of players who did our jobs,

Played clean and fair—and though we win,

Other teams are glad to play us again."

SO . . .

Keep both teams safe, and help us not

To forget the awesome God we've got!

In Your Bible

You can find lots of stories in which people pray to God, and things turn out just as they are supposed to. The stories of Elijah in 1 Kings 17 and 18 are wonderful examples. (If you have *The Growing Reader Phonics Bible,* you can find those stories on pages 163–180.)

A Prayer to See
As God Sees

TO HAVE WISDOM AND UNDERSTANDING

Father, I've heard you're all-knowing, all-wise.
It's as if you have television-like eyes—
The kind that can see in front of your face
At the same time they're seeing a faraway place.
With your vision you see where I am today,
But you also see millions of years away!

I'll never have your vision that's wide
Enough to see way down inside
The thoughts that hide in a heart and mind.
But would you be so very kind
To lend me a bit of heavenly vision
When I need to make a hard decision?

Where there's hurt and confusion, I'll ask you
  for sight
To see what is wrong—then I'll make it right.
When I'm feeling down, give me vision to see
The wonderful treasures you have for me.
And when others mistreat me, Lord, if you would,
Give me eyes of love so I'll see what is good.
If I whine because something's not grand enough,
Please show me the pleasure in just plain stuff!

Like Jesus' disciples who prayed to be wise,
I'll look for your help—and I don't mind
  surprise!

In Your Bible
When Jesus was taken up to heaven, he left his friends with a job to do after Judas's death. They were not sure what decision to make, so they asked for his help. You can read the story in Acts 1:21-26. (If you have *The Growing Reader Phonics Bible,* you can read how God helped his friends on pages 393–400.)

A Prayer for
Our Country

TO SEEK AND DO WHAT IS GOOD AND RIGHT

In the "home of the brave and the land of the
  free"—
That's the place where I live, and I'm thankful to be
Where alone—with just me—or with a big crowd,
I can talk to you quietly OR right out LOUD!
In my room or outside where everyone sees,
I am free to worship you, Lord, as I please.

Dear God in heaven, just what do you see
When your eyes look down on this land that is free,
Where so many people believe in you,
But we often don't live like you ask us to?
We are your people and you are our God.
You have loved us so well, that it would seem odd

If we didn't treat others as
YOU'VE taught us to.
You said, "Love one another as
I have loved you."

Help us share what we have and not be greedy,
Be kind to our neighbors and care for the needy,
And treat each other with friendly respect.
We'll pray for the leaders the grown-ups
  elect—
That they will be wise enough to seek
Your wisdom and power, for they are weak.
But you are strong, and you know best.
Please show them how to lead all the rest.

I pray, as your people, together we might
Teach all of the world what is good and right.
When you look at our country, I hope you will see
Many kids you can count on, including ME!

In Your Bible
You can read how God blessed a country, even when its people grumbled and didn't obey him. And he used just one man (who wasn't even very good at talking) to lead that nation. The story is in Exodus 2:23–4:20; 14:21-22; and 16:1–17:7. (If you have *The Growing Reader Phonics Bible*, you can find this fascinating story on pages 83–88 and 101–105.)

A Nighttime Prayer

WHEN I AM AFRAID IN THE DARK

Sometimes when I go to bed,
I shut my eyes, but in my head
I see imaginary things
With shaggy hair and shimmery wings.
Or silly shapes that shadows make
Seem scary, and I start to shake.

I wish I were a braver kid.
But when I open just one lid
To check it out and take a peek,
Something brushes past my cheek!
Oh no! I feel it in my hair!!!
Whoosh! How silly! It's just fresh air—
A gush that blew my window shut
And nearly made me shout out. BUT . . .

I'm much too old. I can't admit
That I think ghosts and goblins get
In to my room. I'd be ashamed,
And then, of course, I should be named
A scaredy-cat! No one must know it.
I WILL NOT shiver . . . WILL NOT show it!

So God, I'm glad that I can share
With you the silly things that scare
And shock and startle me at night.
I'm thankful you are like a light.
When things are dark, I call on you.
I know you hear. And I know too
You care. And you don't mind that tears
Are sometimes shed with silly fears.
But till I am a little older,
May I snuggle on your shoulder?

Shhh! I think I'm sleepy now. . . .

In Your Bible
If you think *you* are scared of the dark, think about how scared Joseph was in a dark,
scary jail with things creeping around him. It's nice to know that Joseph's story had
a happy ending! Read about it in Genesis 39–41. (If you have *The Growing Reader
Phonics Bible*, you can find this part of Joseph's story on pages 58–64.)

ng

Note: The *ng* sound comes only from the
n in the words *angry* and *think*.
ng as in strong
n as in angry, think

A Prayer for Forgiveness

WHEN I AM ANGRY AND BLOW MY TOP

I'm mad! I'm mad!
I'm very mad!
And I am feeling
Really bad!
I'm like King Saul,
Who behaved like a jerk—
Got angry at David
And went berserk!

Lately, I'm feeling angry a lot,
And I don't like it. I do not!
As with Saul, things happen I cannot stop.
Then bing! Bang! Bong! I blow my top.

I should give thanks. You say it brings
A happy heart, but at such things
As quick forgiveness, I'm not strong—
Somehow I often get it wrong.

So help me, Lord, while I am young
To learn to smile and hold my tongue.
The next time things don't go my way,
I hope that you will hear me say,
"Forgive me, Lord. I'm tickled pink
That I'm beginning now to think
Before I act in angry ways."
And thanks for hearing
me . . . always!

In Your Bible
You can read in
1 Samuel 17:51–20:42
about how King Saul
acted when he was
jealous and angry. (If you
have *The Growing Reader
Phonics Bible*, you can find
Saul's story on pages 150–157.)
In the book of Proverbs, God gives
lots of advice about how to act. (In *The
Growing Reader Phonics Bible*, you can find
some of that advice on pages 214–220.)

er

er as in her
ir as in bird
or as in word
ur as in fur

A Birthday Prayer

FOR GOD'S SPECIAL BLESSING

The last two stanzas on page 78 may be repeated in unison as a group prayer.
Or after the words "In Jesus' dear name, we all say . . ."
everyone can respond with a joyful "Amen!"

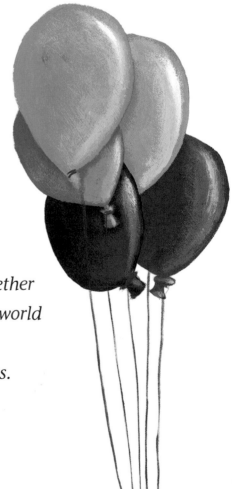

Balloons of circus colors—blue
And red and green and yellow
   too—
Swirling, turning, twirling high,
"Surprise! Surprise!" loud voices
   cry.
Then someone starts, and all
   together,
Everyone sings. No question whether
They know the song. The whole world
   knows!
"Happy Birthday!" is how it goes.

This is the way the party starts—
With a burst of happy in all of our hearts.
And then comes a perfectly scrumptious cake.
As it's cut to order, the server will make

A piece that each guest is certainly sure
Has just enough frosting for him or her.

And then comes the moment we all love best—
The part that is better than all the rest—
When family and friends all gather to bless
The person whose birthday it is. We say, "Yes,
We love you. We bless you. We want you to stay!"
We join in a circle. Together we pray:

Group Prayer:
"To this circle of love, dear Father, please come.
To celebrate now the life of this one.
May your love and care so perfect and tender
Bring peace and joy. May you be (his/her) defender.

"As we hold hands together, please send from above
Your blessing on _____ [say name], whom all
 of us love.
For another year, we thank you!" And then,
"In Jesus' dear name, we all say . . . Amen!"

In Your Bible
You can read, in Matthew 3, the story of God's special blessing on his own Son.
(If you have *The Growing Reader Phonics Bible*, you can find God's words of blessing
on page 277.)

air

ar, air, and are as in
scary, hair, care
er, ear, ere, and eir as in
very, bear, where, their

A Prayer for My Family

WHEN WE ARE SAD AND HURTING

There's a big hurt in our family right now.
We are scared and don't know exactly how
To fix it, Lord. So we need your care.
Without your help we cannot repair
The sadness and every broken part
That's ripping and tearing at each one's heart.

There's a Bible story I've heard before
Where big family troubles nearly tore
Twelve brothers and their parent apart,
And a pair of lies broke the father's heart.
Their troubles were not the very same kind
As ours, but their family was on your mind.

Lord, even when they were mean and unfair,
You held them and kept them safe in your care.
And you used their hurts to prepare them, then
You brought them all back together again.

I know I can dare to count on you
To take good care of MY family too.
I'm thankful that you are very, very
Extra "extra-ordinary."
And you're a good listener too!

In Your Bible

Can you guess the name of the family in the Bible story? Look up Genesis 37 to see if you are right. (If you have *The Growing Reader Phonics Bible*, you will find the whole story about this family on pages 53–74. It's a long story, but it has a happy ending!)

k

k as in kind
c as in come
ck as in truck

A Prayer of Thanksgiving

FOR GOD'S UNCONDITIONAL LOVE

A kid like me is loved by parents
And grandparents, cousins, and friends.
But, Lord, you love me even better
'Cuz I know your love never ends.

Your Word says I am one of a kind.
You track every thought in my head.
And though you take care of thousands of kids,
You count every tear that I shed.

I'm made in your image—a picture of you—
So you know just what to expect.
You want me to copy your perfect ways,
Though often I don't. I neglect
To keep connected in conversation.
You must feel rejected and sad.
I act like I'm off on a long vacation
From you, but you never
  get mad.

You take me back and you're quick to forgive.
You comfort me when I'm confused.
My cantankerous ways you seem to forget,
And my clumsy mistakes are excused.

You make my heart DANCE with the sound of
music,
My smile comes back. Then soon—
Quick as a wink—I'm humming a hymn
Or singing a catchy tune.

My Creator, my God, my Comforter, Friend,
My Lord with a capital L,
My Shepherd, Encourager, Caretaker, King—
I thank you for loving me well!

In Your Bible
Read about the day God made people—on the sixth day of his creation—in Genesis
1:26-31. (If you have *The Growing Reader Phonics Bible*, you can read the story on
pages 12–18.)

An Evening Prayer

AFTER SOMETHING GRAND HAS HAPPENED

Fantastic! Bombastic! Lord, how can I say
Thank you for all you have done today?
I know you are good at a difficult task,
But sometimes you give me much more than I ask.
I guess I am feeling the same special joy
That Sarah and Abraham felt when their boy
Arrived after all of those years that they waited.
How happy they were as they celebrated!

Perhaps an answer far grander than grand
Was saved for two sisters the day your Son planned
To honor you as he called from the dead
Their brother Lazarus. And then the news spread

That One with such power was not really odd
But was, in fact, the dear Son of God.

I'm glad that these dazzling stories of old
Are not the only fantastic ones told.
For it is your habit, still, as the master
Of everything good, to change a disaster
To something astonishing, so all will see
That your answers to prayer bring good things
   to be.

I thank you, dear God, for your gifts and surprises,
Which usually come in gargantuan sizes.
And not just to people who lived long ago,
But to kids like me and the people I know.

In Your Bible
You can read the exciting story about Sarah and Abraham in Genesis 15:5;
17:17-19; 21:1-7 and about Lazarus in John 11:1-45. (If you have *The Growing
Reader Phonics Bible*, you will find Sarah and Abraham dancing in the story on
pages 34–39 and Lazarus coming out of his grave on pages 345–351.)

A Prayer of Celebration

ON THE ARRIVAL OF A NEW BABY

A new little child has joined us! Oh, boy!
The baby arrived. We're excited! What joy!
Oh, Lord, I thank you that babies' sweet voices
Make all of us smile. The whole family rejoices.
We're busy, we're tired, and sometimes annoyed
With our baby. But, Father, we're still overjoyed!

So now I am wondering: Could it just be
That you send each child to an earth family,
To remind us all from heaven afar
How absolutely amazing you are?
Are you making the point that you still create
All life, which humans cannot duplicate?

I might be wrong, but I think you are saying,

"Remember when Joseph and Mary were staying

One night in a borrowed Bethlehem shed,

And heavenly voices joyfully said,

'Glory to God in the highest! Rejoice!

And peace to the earth.'" For it was your choice

To send to us heaven's royal King

As a baby boy who would someday bring

Us joy. Oh yes! Jesus' birth excites us.

And the life of each new girl and boy delights us.

So together our family says, "Father above,

Thanks for our noisy package of love!"

In Your Bible
Read the joyful stories of new babies that came to Hannah in 1 Samuel 1 and to Ruth and Boaz—and especially Grandma Naomi—in the book of Ruth. (If you have *The Growing Reader Phonics Bible*, you can find these stories on pages 130–138 and 123–129.)

A Prayer for God's Help

WHEN I FEEL LIKE MY HEART IS BROKEN

Dear Father, I'm broken, down deep in my heart.
I'm sad, and I feel like I'm falling apart.
It's like being lost in the dark at night,
Where there isn't even one star in sight.

You know what to do, Lord, when things go bad.
When sin spoiled your beautiful world, you were
  sad,
And so you took charge and did something smart
To give the world a fresh new start.
You chose a hardworking, strong-armed man
Who was sharp and wise, and you made a plan.
"Hey, Noah, come be my partner," you said.
"And don't be alarmed—I'm not out of my head,

But I want you to do something very hard.
Build an ark right out in your own backyard!"

When I'm not crying, I'm thinking a lot
About what to do. But it's hard—and
  I'm not
Very good at getting myself restarted.
    You are famous for being kindhearted.
    I've read Noah's story, so I know that you
      Are the best choice for making me feel like new.
        Please be my partner and help me start
        To mend the pieces of my broken heart.
          And, Lord, I can hardly wait to see
            How you're going to bring
              new life to me.

In Your Bible
Genesis 6:5-6 talks about how disappointed God was that sinful
people were spoiling his beautiful world. It says, "So the Lord was
sorry he had ever made them. It broke his heart." (If you have *The
Growing Reader Phonics Bible,* you can read the whole story about
Noah. Read how God used him to make the world new and fresh
again and heal the hurt in God's heart. The story is on pages 24–33.)

A Prayer for God's Help

WHEN I AM LONELY

Dear God, do you ever feel alone?
I suppose you don't because you own
The whole world you made long ago.
But the Son you sent to earth had to go
To a cross alone. And his best friends lied,
Saying, "No, we don't know him!" and ran to hide.
So if anyone understands, you do—
Since it happened to someone so close to you.

When I feel lonely, it's good to know
That you are with me wherever I go—

Especially at times when, under my skin,
Is a kid who's afraid and doesn't fit in
Or needs a friend who will call on the phone,
Saying "Come to my house for an
ice-cream cone!"

But I'm never REALLY alone—any day
'Cuz you are only a prayer away!
Thanks, God, for being my friend. . . . By the way,
A moment alone is a nice time
   to pray!

In Your Bible
You can read about a very lonely time in the life
of God's Son, Jesus, in John 18–19. (If you have
The Growing Reader Phonics Bible, you will find
the story on pages 371–377.)

u

u as in cube
ew as in few
ou as in you

A Prayer of Thanksgiving

FOR THE PRIVILEGE OF CONVERSATION WITH GOD

It's you and me, God—just us two.

Just little me—and great, huge you.

I am human. You are God.

And I agree, it's very odd

From many another person's view.

But in your Word, you say it's true

That we can talk—just us together,

AND it doesn't matter whether

I am young and don't know how

To talk to you with "thee" and "thou."

Just let me take my cues from you,

And help me see YOUR point of view.

Like Samuel whom you called at night,
I try to listen and do what's right,

ugh sometimes I am more like Cain
nd just don't get it—don't use my brain.
But you continue to love me so,
To talk to me and help me know
To you I'm as valuable as gold.
And still, in the future, when I am old,
I'm glad we will be a duet—a pair—
Who can talk any time and anywhere.

In Your Bible
Read the story of Samuel's duet with God in 1 Samuel 3. (If you have *The Growing Reader Phonics Bible*, you can find the beginning of the story on page 130.)

A Together Table Prayer

THANKSGIVING FOR GOD'S INVENTION OF TASTY FOODS

Genesis 1:29

One person may read all the parts of this prayer, or several people may take one or more parts. An entire group or family may read together each response marked "All."

Speaker 1: *"I give you every*
plant and tree—
Yours for food."
How happily
We've received your splendid
plan
Of healthy meals since time began.

All: *We join our hands. Our heads are*
bowed.
Together, in one voice, aloud,
We thank you for our daily bread,
O Lord, by whose kind hand we're fed.

Speaker 2: *No one but you could have ever invented*
So many tastes to keep us contented.

Speaker 3: *Who else would have thought of trees making fruits,*
Or corn, beans, and berries that start from roots?

All: *We join our hands. Our heads are bowed.*
Together, in one voice, aloud,
We thank you for our daily bread,
O Lord, by whose kind hand we're fed.

Speaker 4: *You make COWS
that give milk for butters
and creams.
You grow FISH for my dinner
in cold mountain streams.*

112

Speaker 5: *Small seeds*
become pumpkins.
And chickens with legs
Can pop out of roundish,
brown-speckled eggs.

All: *We join our hands. Our heads are bowed.*

Together, in one voice, aloud,

We thank you for our daily bread,

O Lord, by whose kind hand we're fed.

Speaker 1: *Now we can't imagine a human brain*

That could think up a way to create a grain

That someone could turn into cinnamon toast

Or Pop-Tarts or Cheerios—you are the MOST!!!

All: *We join our hands. Our heads are bowed.*

Together, in one voice, aloud,

We thank you for our daily bread,

O Lord, by whose kind hand we're fed.

In Your Bible

If you would like to read about the days of creation when God made foods of all kinds, you can look in Genesis 1:1–2:3, 18-23. (If you have *The Growing Reader Phonics Bible*, you will find the story on pages 8–18.)

A Prayer for Healing

WHEN A LOVED ONE IS SICK

I love my Bible storybook
With tales so wild and strange.
But there's an ugly story that
I really would like to change.
It happened in a garden one day—
A lovely, beautiful place—
Until a sly and slippery serpent
Showed his clever face.

That serpent was bad,
That serpent was sly,
That serpent told Eve
A terrible lie.

And because she and Adam
   believed that lie,
And did what God said
   not to do,
Sin and sickness came
   into the world
And created a
   hullabaloo.
      (That's a
         mess.)
And since that
   day, there's
   been much
   sadness
And sickness,
   and people die.
And it's all the fault
   of that devil snake
Who told the
   terrible lie.

But, Lord, you are more powerful
Than any silly snake.
And you can heal and help us when
We're ill with pain or ache.
And even when the medicines
Don't work, you know
just how
To make our bodies well
and whole.
And so I ask you
now—
As you helped the
man who came
on his mat
Down through a
roof one day,

And who told many people how Jesus made
Him so well, he could walk away—
Please listen, Lord, to this very, very,
VERY serious request
To heal someone I love a lot,

For I'm sure that you know best
Exactly how to help. So may
Your perfect will be done.
And now I'll whisper to you
the name—
Dear Lord, please heal this
one.

In Your Bible

Read the ugly, sad story of the serpent in
Genesis 2 and 3, and the story of the sick
man in Mark 2:1-12. (If you have *The
Growing Reader Phonics Bible*, you can find
the serpent story on pages 19–23 and the
one about the happy man Jesus healed
on pages 286–291.)

A Prayer about Peace and Safety

WHEN THERE IS A STORM

Whenever the sky is dark and gray
And I hear the wind whine and whistle, I say
A secret prayer, and I think of the trip
When a great, wild storm began to whip
Like a whirlwind against the small white sail
Of a boat, and a bunch of disciples turned pale

And held on for dear
  life while big waves
  whacked
The side of the boat, and cold
  water smacked
Their faces. And Jesus was asleep.
"Wake up!" they whimpered. "The
  storm will sweep
Us overboard, and we all will drown!"
But there was no need to worry
  or frown.
Jesus spoke—maybe
  whispered—"Peace!
  Be still!"
And the wind and the
  waters obeyed his will.

What a scare! What a whopper that
storm was. Whew!
But then the disciples certainly knew

That this man was the Son of
   God. And when
I read about them in the
   Bible, then
I learned to believe
   that I can just
Relax when a
   storm comes.
   I can trust

That the God who could
stop a wind that hard
Can handle the storms
in my backyard.

So, Lord, I'm
thankful I'm
safe in your care
No matter
what
storm
comes
from
anywhere.

In Your Bible
Read the story of the
scary storm in Luke
8:22-25. (If you have
*The Growing Reader
Phonics Bible*, it will be
fun to read "Who Can
Stop a Scary Storm
with Just a Shout?"
on pages 306–313.)

A Morning Prayer

THOUGHTS ON HOW TO SAY I LOVE GOD

I've been thinking, dear Father, about some way
To tell you I love you, rather than say
Just words, 'cuz I don't know very many.
It bothered me not to come up with any
Other good ways that would let you know
How I feel about you. But then I said, "Whoa!"

You gave us some rules that show us the way
To love you and others. One says to obey
Your father and mother. Another says not
To think any thing or person you've got
In your life is more important than God—
At first that idea seemed very odd,

Till I thought how often I'd rather do
A million things other than talk to you.
Neither am I very good at forgiving—
That's one other rule you gave for good living.
And I'm often slow at helping others,
Even my friends and sisters and brothers.

But thank you for being so very kind
By putting together some thoughts in my mind
That will help me, even withOUT words, to show
Your love to all of the people I know.

And just to prove that I am sincere,
See other ideas I've gathered here:

- Love your neighbor as yourself. Matthew 22:39
- If you love me, obey my commandments. John 14:15
- Be kind to each other . . . forgiving one another. Ephesians 4:32
- Share with others. 1 Timothy 6:18

Okay! Okay! So I'm the worst—
Of course these were YOUR ideas first!

In Your Bible
If you want to know how to love God better, you can read some of his important commandments in Exodus 20:1-17 (the Ten Commandments) and in Matthew 22:37-39 (the two greatest commandments). (If you have *The Growing Reader Phonics Bible*, you'll find the whole story of how God gave the Ten Commandments to Moses on pages 106–114.)

A Prayer for Missionaries

FOR THOSE WHO CARRY GOD'S MESSAGE TO OTHERS

Lord, sometimes you ask your people to go
Away from their homes and the places they know
To take your message to lands that seem strange,
Where much of what they've been used to will
change.

I can't imagine the
courage it takes
To go to a village where there are
huge snakes,
Or where people believe that things
evil and odd—
Like magic—are more important
than God,
Where no one has heard of your
wonderful plan;
They think Jesus was just a regular
man.

But most of us, Father, you ask
to stay
In the town we've been used
to every day,

130

Where the people we
  meet understand
  each word,
But your message of love, they may not
  have heard.
Though they live where there usually
  isn't much danger,
Their friends and
  family don't know
  the manger

Was the place for the very special birth
Of your only Son, Jesus, who came to earth
To die so that every person who would
Be glad to believe in him, someday could
Be ready to join in the celebration
In heaven. Your personal invitation
Is open to all. But there's work to be done
If the whole world is going to hear of your Son,
Whom you love so much. So you ask us to pray
For those who are near us and those far away,
Who carry your message of joy and great love
To people who don't know the Father above.

So please send your angels to watch over all
Your missionaries, so they, just like Paul
And Silas, the night they were thrown into jail,
May know your gigantic love cannot fail.

In Your Bible
Read the hair-raising story of Paul and Silas in Acts 16:16-34. (If you have *The Growing Reader Phonics Bible*, you will find their story on pages 408–413.)

oo

oo as in look
u as in push
ou as in could

A Together Prayer of Worship

TO CELEBRATE GOD'S GOODNESS

Verses may be read by one person or
by several individuals. Everyone can join
on the two-line refrain.

Speaker 1: *Praise to my*
God, for he is good.
No one else in the whole
world would
Send his Son to a cross made of wood
To die for me. How I wish I could
Become a child who wants to learn
To love God fully in return.

All: *Let's praise the Lord together as*
we should,
With joyful hearts, for he is good!

135

Speaker 2: He pushes no-good people away
But loves each one who is willing to say,
"I believe!" And in his Book
He puts these words: "Just come and look
To me, and you'll be safe forever.
I WILL not leave you. Never, NEVER!"

All: Let's praise the Lord together as we should,
With joyful hearts, for he is good!

Speaker 3: Healer of hurts and hearts that
   are sad,
Listener to
   prayers—my
   heavenly Dad,
Savior, Good Shepherd,
   Master, and King,
Creator and Lord of every
   good thing.
No one can pull or push us apart,
For I have given to you my heart.

All: Let's praise the Lord
   together as we should,
With joyful hearts, for he
   is good!

In Your Bible
The verse where God says "look to me" is Isaiah 45:22. In Matthew 28:20 Jesus promises he will always be with us. The story about the Cross is in John 19. Stories about Jesus the Healer are found in Matthew 8 and 9. (If you have *The Growing Reader Phonics Bible*, you can read those stories on pages 278–291.)

A Prayer for Help and Forgiveness

WHEN I HAVE DISOBEYED

Children, obey your parents because you belong to the Lord, for this is the right thing to do. "Honor your father and mother." This is the first of the Ten Commandments that ends with a promise. And this is the promise: If you honor your father and mother, "you will live a long life, full of blessing." Ephesians 6:1-3

You ask me to honor my parents. I bet

That I can't do it, Lord—and yet,

If I say yes and try to obey,

Your commandment promises I will stay

Alive beyond my expected years,

And I won't need to have any fears,

For things will go well—I'll be safe in your care.

And though I think that is more than fair—

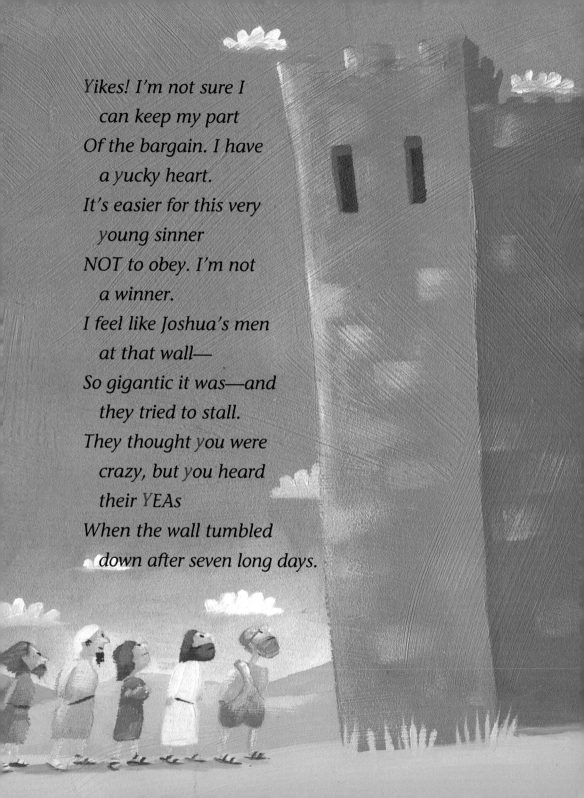

Yikes! I'm not sure I
   can keep my part
Of the bargain. I have
   a yucky heart.
It's easier for this very
   young sinner
NOT to obey. I'm not
   a winner.
I feel like Joshua's men
   at that wall—
So gigantic it was—and
   they tried to stall.
They thought you were
   crazy, but you heard
   their YEAs
When the wall tumbled
   down after seven long days.

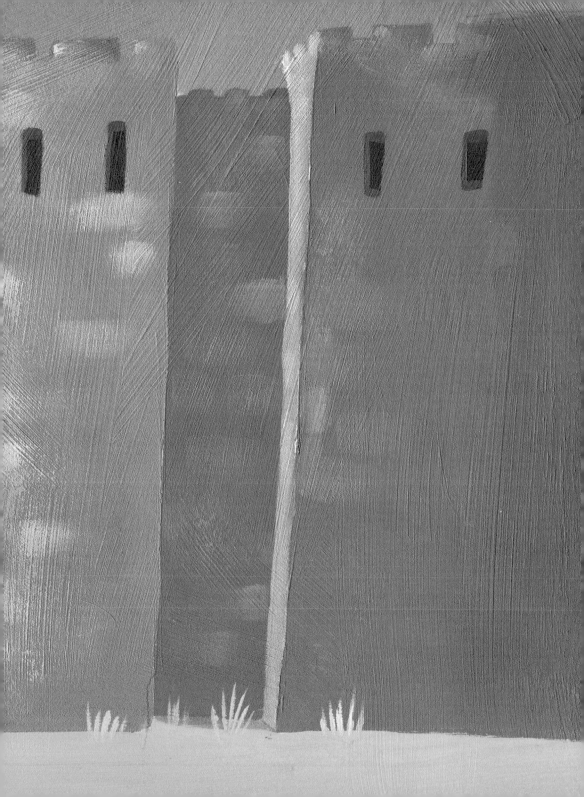

Lord, what you're asking, I promise that I'll
    Work hard at, but every once in
      a while,
      You may have to yank or yelp
        or yowl
        'Cuz that old snake Satan is still
        on the prowl.
      And just when I plan to do
      something good,
That yo-yo starts teasing, "Don't do
    what you should!"
He yaps and he yaks till he gets control,
And I feel like crawling into a hole.

I am so ashamed. Yet you carry me out,
And then I can almost hear you shout,
"I love you! I love you! You're precious to me.
You're young, but not yucky, and you can be
Forgiven and have a heart clean and new,
And everything else I have planned for you!"

Thank you, dear God! And thank you again
For rescuing me from my sins. Amen.

In Your Bible

Read Joshua 6 to see how God responds to his people when they obey—even after
they grumble and make fun of their leader and don't believe they can do what God
asks them to. (If you have *The Growing Reader Phonics Bible*, you can read the story
on pages 115–122.)

A Prayer for God's Help

WHEN SOMEONE DIES

God blesses those who mourn, for they will be comforted. Matthew 5:4

Dear Lord, I'm young but smart enough
To know that you are good.
But death I do not understand,
So please, Lord, if you would,
Come, help my mixed-up mind to know
Exactly how to feel
When someone I love very much
Has died. It's so unreal
That I cannot imagine life
Without this one so dear.
It seems there will be no more fun,
No merry times—no cheer.

So I am sad and sort of mad
And hurt. I wish I knew
Just what you mean when
  you say, "Come,
And I will comfort you!"
I know you've made a special home
In heaven for all those
Who love you and believe in you.
So someday, I suppose,
Though now it's hard to say good-bye,
Once more we'll be together.
And maybe then, my heart again
Will feel light as a feather.

You promise in heaven that we will never
Be lonely or sad or afraid.
We will not be sick or cry or die
In that marvelous place you've made.
And here on earth, you promise us peace
And comfort. So I'm in your care.
I know I'm still going to miss very much
The one who is gone, but I'll dare

To trust your Word and believe that maybe
The time will come in a while
When things will again seem to be okay.
You might even see me smile.

And in the meantime, I thank you, Lord,
That you are a God of might
Who can turn my hurts and problems around
Into something good and right,
And give good memories for me to keep,
And make my future bright.

P.S. I love you!

In Your Bible

Read Matthew 5:4 and Psalm 23 to see how God gives comfort to those who are sad and hurting. (If you have *The Growing Reader Phonics Bible*, you will love reading a story about what heaven is like—"The Best 'Happily Ever After' Ever!" You can find it on pages 414–421. The story is based on Revelation 21.)

A Prayer for Those Who Are Poor

ASKING GOD TO SHOW ME HOW TO HELP

When I was a baby, I had a crib,

Bottles and balls and a fancy bib

With ribbons, a teddy bear to hug,

And blankets to keep me warm and snug.

But bunches of children are not like me.

For most of the time, my family

Has gobs of stuff that we don't even need,

While many big families cannot feed

Their children—their fridge and cupboards are bare.

They have no boots and no robes to wear.

The parents lost jobs and don't have any

Money for bills—not even a penny!

So, Lord, I've been thinking what I could do
To help somebody—but unlike you,
Who made the widow's oil and flour
Fill up each day, I have no power
To make big troubles go away.
But if I can help someone today,
When I'm done talking, please be so kind
As to put good thoughts into my mind,
And help me know the best thing to do
To be a good friend and honor you.

In Your Bible
In Elijah's time, God did amazing things to help people with troubles. You can read about them in 1 Kings 17. (If you have *The Growing Reader Phonics Bible*, you will find those stories on pages 168–171.) If you would like to see how God treats people with special needs—still, today—read Psalm 146.

A Together Prayer on Easter Morning

TO CELEBRATE THE RISEN CHRIST

One person may read all the parts of this prayer, or several people
may take one or more parts. An entire group or family
may read together the stanzas marked "All."

All: He's alive! Christ is risen—just as he said.

He's alive! Yes, Jesus is no longer dead!

Speaker 1: This hair-raising story of Easter morning,

When up from the grave Jesus rose without warning,

We celebrate here on this fine Easter day

And worship the risen Christ as we pray.

All: He's alive! Christ is risen—just as he said.

He's alive! Yes, Jesus is no longer dead!

Speaker 2: *We thank you, Lord God, for your
   mighty power*
That shook the earth in that early hour
On Sunday morning when angels appeared
And just what Jesus' enemies feared
Might happen DID! The stone from the grave
Was rolled away. And the angel gave
Good news to the women who came to see:
"Surprise! The grave is empty," said he,
"For Jesus is risen. Go tell his friends!"
Hallelujah! We love how this story ends.

All: *He's alive! Christ is risen—just as he said.*
He's alive! Yes, Jesus is no longer dead!

Speaker 3: *We're excited just as your friends were
   that day,*
For it's your resurrection that makes the way
For every person who loves you to go
To heaven. And when we all get there, we know
Our celebration will be even better,
For that PARTY will be a doubleheader.

Speaker 4: *All those who love you will be together*
Again, and so it won't matter whether
We've already died or are still alive
When you come to get us. We'll all arrive
Where everything will be bright and new.
But best of all, we will be there with you!

Hallelujah! We love how this NEW story ends!
Since Jesus is risen, we'll tell all our friends.

All: He's alive! Christ is risen—just as he said.
He's alive! Praise God! He is no longer dead!

In Your Bible
Read the exciting story of the first Easter morning in Matthew 27:62–28:10. (If you
have *The Growing Reader Phonics Bible*, you can find the story on pages 378–385.)

An Evening Prayer

FOR FORGIVENESS BECAUSE I OFTEN
DON'T PRAY AS I OUGHT

Lord, I've been thinking about what I do
So often when I am talking to you.
I sound like I'm walking through a mall
With a great, long shopping list of all
The things I want. And then I pout
If I don't get them, or I doubt
That you can hear me. So I say,
"It doesn't matter if I pray.
Perhaps God's busy, and he's missed
My call—or maybe he's lost my list.
I'll never get that fancy bike
Or those special tennis shoes I like.
My paper won't have an A by my name,
And I'm sure my ball team will lose the game."

Then I get cross. "Stop making a fuss,"
I say. "Hey, God's not Toys "R" Us.
And he's not playing Santa Claus!"
Then I feel awful, and I pause.
My silly thoughts have gone all wrong.
Of course, you were listening all along.
For you're not like that god they call Baal,
Whose prophets had to bawl and wail
To get attention. You are right
Where we can talk both day and night.

And so, forgive the times I've brought
Such selfish prayers—I guess I caught
The Gimme-This and Gimme-That
Disease. I came off like a brat.
And worse, I lost that time with you.
(It's awesome when it's just us two.)
So I need you, Lord, to please help me
Wake up each morning thinking WE!

In Your Bible
You can see the difference between the living God and false gods like Baal if you
read the story of Elijah's contest with 450 prophets. It is in 1 Kings 18. (If you have
The Growing Reader Phonics Bible, you can find the story on pages 172–180.)

A Table Prayer for Thanksgiving Day

TO PRAY TOGETHER WITH FAMILY AND FRIENDS

Ephesians 5:20

Everyone may speak or sing the hymn together. The other stanzas
may be read around the table, with each person taking a turn.

Hymn: Now thank we all our God,
With heart and hands and voices,
Who wondrous things hath done,
In whom His world rejoices.

Thanksgiving day! So full of delights:
The smells and colors, sounds and sights.

The spicy scent of turkey stuffing,
Dinner rolls in the oven puffing.

A turkey with its thick, brown skin,
Its big fat breast with wings tucked in.

The sugary crust on an apple pie,
And dozens of cookies, stacked three high.

Tables all dressed for the holiday
In white linen cloth and silver tray.

Dinner so late you could starve to death,
Then eating so much you can't get your breath.

After the fourth or fifth helping, "Oh, WHY
Did I do this?" you say. "I'm going to die!"

But you don't—instead, you declare it delicious
And hope you won't have to help with the dishes.

There's a joyful feeling of family,
Talking and laughing and happy to be
Loving each other through thick and thin
While Baby is showing a toothy grin.

And everyone huddles, both young and old,
To listen to stories that have been told

A *thousand* times. But all the way through
We laugh and cry as if they were new.

As the holiday ends, each person will know
The truth is that we are blessed. And so,
With grateful hearts, we pause to share
Our thoughts. Please hear this
    simple prayer:

Hymn: Now thank we all our God,
With heart and hands and voices,
Who wondrous things hath done,
In whom His world rejoices.

In Your Bible:
To read about the thanksgiving celebration the children of Israel
had after they crossed the Red Sea, see Exodus 14:1–15:21. (If you
have *The Growing Reader Phonics Bible*, you
will find the story on pages 95–100.)

oo

oo as in moon
ue as in true
ew as in new
ough as in through

A Prayer That I Will Be Quick to Pray

WHEN OTHERS NEED HELP

Sometimes things happen—just out of the blue
When no one ever expected them to.
And when it appears that these things are not
So good, then a prayer said right on the spot
Could help somebody get safely through
A hurtful or harmful bugaboo.

Lord, I'm going to count on you
To remind me—help me get your cue
When I see someone in distress
Or there is some unusual mess:
A fire, a storm, an accident,
A fight, a shooting, an argument;

173

Someone in a nasty mood,
Someone hungry without food,
Someone hot who needs some COOL,
A kid who is suddenly sick at school,
Or an unsuspecting kid who's new
And gets hit by a bully—a sockeroo!

A tired dad,
A mom who's had
A day that's tough
With worry stuff,
A baby crying,
Someone dying.

For anyone who's in danger or trouble,
I want to zoom in—and on the double!
As soon as I'm able, I'll be on alert
To call on you to smooth the hurt.
I want to be like Moses' mother
And his sister who watched her baby brother.
When he was in danger, they listened to you,
And look at the things Moses grew up to do!

We live in an unpredictable zoo,

So it's very nice to know it is true

That you are pleased when we help a brother.

You have commanded us, "Love one another."

And I want to follow in your way,

So use me, Lord. Make me quick to pray.

In Your Bible
Because Moses' mother and sister were alert and listening for God's cues, the baby Moses was saved from danger. He grew up and let God use him to lead God's children to the Promised Land. Read the story in Exodus 1:8–2:10. (If you have *The Growing Reader Phonics Bible*, you can find this happy story on pages 75–82.)

A Prayer for God's Help

ABOUT MY JOB AT SCHOOL

A long time ago, in Abraham's day,
He called to his servant and sent him away
To do a job—a special one:
To find a wife for Abraham's son.
Off went the servant. He would
  not stop
Till his job was done for Isaac's pop.
He would look for a lady to be Isaac's wife—
Someone to love Isaac all of his life.

While the servant was willing, the job was hard.
So he was barely out of the yard

177

When he prayed, "O Lord, please help me find
The right girl for Isaac." Then into his mind
Came a whopper idea. He could not wait
To try God's plan. Well, the plan was great!
And everything worked just like a charm.
The happy couple walked arm in arm
After their wedding. The servant smiled.
"Good job, God!" he said. "Your idea was wild!"
It would never have worked for the servant alone,
But YOUR plan was perfect. He should have known!

I, too, have a job, Lord. I'll have it for years.
It's to be a good student. But worries and fears
Wear me out, and worse—they often make
It so hard my tummy begins to ache.
When I can't do my work, I do stupid things
Till the bell for recess finally rings.

So I need your help to do my job.
Please help me not to be a slob

And waste my time just watching the clock
Or sitting around like a wooden block.
And I pray, dear God, you will give me wings
To fly through my homework when other things—
Like walking the dog or watching TV—
Always seem to be calling to me.

Wake up my brain and make me wise.
Please help me to watch with wide-awake eyes
And listen well to every direction
And take advantage of my connection
To you, who would like me to do my best—
Not worry, but study to pass each test,
And never feel stupid or weird or weak
When all that I have to do is speak:
"Lord, may I, like Abraham's servant, be
Good at the job you have chosen for me."

In Your Bible
The strange and wonderful story of how God helped Abraham's servant do his job is in Genesis 24. (If you have *The Growing Reader Phonics Bible*, you will find the story on pages 40–46.)

A Morning Prayer

A PROMISE TO SPEND TIME WITH GOD

When you pray, go away by yourself, shut the door behind you,
and pray to your Father secretly. Matthew 6:6

It's morning again, Lord. Alone in my bed,

I like to imagine a good day ahead.

And I want to announce as I lie here awake

On this brand new day, that I plan to make

Some special time just for you and me

To be all alone. Don't you agree

That when we're alone, I pay better attention?

In fact, in your Word, I believe you mention

That praying in secret, away and apart

From everything else, is very smart.

Nothing to bother. No one to annoy—

Just time together for us to enjoy.

And I notice that almost every good friend
Of yours in the Bible, beginning to end—
Abraham, Moses, David, and all
The prophets, and people like Mary and Paul,
Joseph and Hannah and Daniel too—
Spent part of each day just talking to you.

So I'll put time aside, away from TV,
For listening awhile as you're talking to me.
And early each morning when day is still new,
I'll be awake—and talking with you.

In Your Bible

One person who spent time talking with God every day was Daniel. Read his story in
Daniel 6. (If you have *The Growing Reader Phonics Bible*, you will find his story on
pages 231–237.)

S

Note: The letter *S* is not always in color in this prayer because it often makes a *Z* sound instead of an *S* sound.

s as in song, c as in city

A Christmas Prayer

ON THE EVE OF CHRIST'S BIRTHDAY

Christmas Eve is finally here.
The city is full of holiday cheer.
And every year on this night in December,
There's something special I like to remember.
It happened in a place that is very hard
To imagine. But often a Christmas card
And Christmas picture books will tell
Its famous story very well.

The place is a barn in Bethlehem town,
Where the stars are brightly shining down,
And out in a pasture dark and chilly,
Some sleepy shepherds are frightened silly
When a host of angel voices sing
Glory to a new little King!

I've always thought it a wondrous sight—
The shepherds hurrying through the night
To the quiet stable—a cozy place
With cows smiling down on the baby's face.
And Mary, his mother so sweet and mild,
Is singing softly to her child.

On second thought, stables are NOT the best
Choice of place for a child to rest.
Lying on prickly, stickly hay
Certainly isn't any way

To get to sleep—and imagine the noise!
Not even a holy family enjoys
A zoo of beasts with swishing tails,
Stomping and chomping and slurping from pails—
A place full of squiggly, wiggly pests,
Crowded with far too many guests,
Like shepherds and sheep with smelly fleece—
An unlikely place for the Prince of Peace!

Instead of a stable, crowded and cold,
One would think he should come to a palace of gold.

But not HIM! Nothing fancy! Not even a smitch
Of ANY thing snazzy or splashy or rich.

And that's why I love to think about
This story. There isn't any doubt
That God sent his Son to earth to be
A part of EVERY family.
For if he had come like a powerful king
With velvety robes and a diamond ring,
Most people would have been very sure
That he couldn't possibly love someone poor.
So he came to our world without anything
And loved us so well that his offering
Of eternal life can be given free
To EVERYONE—yes, even to me.

And that's the story I love to remember
On this joyous evening in December.
And, Lord, I like to believe that just maybe
When you sent your Son as a sweet little baby
To a crowded barn on that starry night,
You were thinking of me. (I bet I'm right!)

So I thank you, Lord. And I welcome you.
And, oh, I forgot . . . Happy birthday too!

In Your Bible
On Christmas Eve, you might enjoy reading the Christmas story in Luke 2:1-20 to
your whole family. (If you have *The Growing Reader Phonics Bible,* you can find the
story told in words and pictures on pages 254–261.)

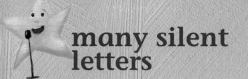

many silent letters

e as in place, gh as in right,
h as in honor, k and w
as in know, l as in talk,
t as in listen, w as in wrong

The Lord's Prayer

THE PRAYER JESUS TAUGHT HIS DISCIPLES TO PRAY

Matthew 6:9-13; Luke 11:1-4

To our Daddy, who lives in a perfect place:
From earth we're not able to see your face.
But we know that you love us. We feel your care.
From heaven, you listen to every prayer.

Honor and glory to you we bring,
O Mighty Maker of every thing.

You must be sad about bad things we do,
But when you come back, ALL things will be new.
So we wait for this evil to pass away
And for you to return—such a happy day!

We have messed up your earth. Now this is not good.
And we do not obey your commands as we should.
We ignore your advice. We worry and fight.
How we wish it might be as you planned it—just right!

All that we have has come from you—
The sun and rain, our breakfast too.

You give the clothing that we wear.
Today this is our quiet prayer:
Give what we need—that is enough.
(But thank you for the extra stuff!)

Sometimes when we kneel to pray
A sigh comes with the words we say,
Because we know the wrong we've done
And bad things over good have won.
But you forgive, then close your eyes
To our mistakes. O God so wise,
To those who wrong me, I would be
As kind as you have been to me.

Down here on earth, things get confusing
And we are not so good at choosing.
It's hard to tell the wrong from right.
But you have said that you are Light,
So please, Lord, shine your beam this way.
Show us our faults. And help us stay
Connected to our heavenly Dad—
Away from stuff we know is bad.

We may have done our best to be good,
But you are the only person who could

Be perfect. We honor you, give you praise.

Your power and glory, we worship always.

Bravo to our hero! Your name we will bless

Forever and ever and ever. Oh yes!

Yes! Yes! Yes!

In Your Bible

This is the prayer Jesus taught his disciples to pray. The many silent letters should remind us to wait quietly after we have talked to God—to be silent as we listen for his answers to us. You can find this prayer in your Bible in two different places: Matthew 6:9-13 and Luke 11:1-4. (If you have *The Growing Reader Phonics Bible,* you'll find it on pages 301–305.)

A Prayer of Worship and Thanksgiving

IN CELEBRATION OF GOD'S POWER

O Lord, my God, I want to shout.

May you be pleased to hear me out.

You made people for your pleasure

So I bow now—just to treasure

Who you are and the things you've done,

And to thank you that I have begun

To praise the name of Jesus aloud—

Let everyone know that I am proud

To be your child and to know your Son,

Who brought your love to everyone.

Astounding—the stories that followed him 'round

From town to town as people found

That he gave them life through his Father's power
And loved them in their darkest hour.
When they were sick and needed rest,
Then he was at his very best,
Helping and healing and teaching each crowd.
How much they loved him, and they bowed
To worship him and seek him out.
But then their leaders began to doubt
That he was the Son of God. They frowned
And ran your name right into the ground.
What lies they told! What trouble they made!
Soon everyone became afraid.
And the crowds began to shout, "Crucify!"
And they led him away to a cross to die.

Well, they thought he was dead—over and out!
But they were not ready for what was about
To happen. Your power shook the ground.
In the place Christ was buried, no body was found.
Astonished, the people ran in fear
When an angel told them: "He is not here!"

Your power had raised him from the dead.

Then the news began to spread:

This Christ was God's beloved Son,

Who died to save us—every one.

The crowds had gotten the story all wrong,

And my telling of it is getting too long,

But one thing I'll never get tired of

Is hearing the story of your great love.

And someday I know that your power will bring

Me to heaven, your home—the home of

  my King!

In Your Bible

The stories in Matthew, Mark, Luke, and John tell all about the wonderful things Jesus did to show his heavenly Father's power. Jesus' teaching began when he was just a child, talking to the leaders at the Temple. That story is in Luke 2:41-52. (If you have *The Growing Reader Phonics Bible*, you can find the whole story of Jesus' life on earth on pages 254–392.) Choose a different story to read each day for a while. You will enjoy seeing God's power at work!

Topical Index of Prayers

PRAYERS OF THANKSGIVING
to celebrate God's gifts of good things **7**
for God's gifts of food **22**
for God's unconditional love **83**
after something grand has happened **88**
on the arrival of a new baby **92**
for the privilege of conversation with God **104**
for God's invention of tasty foods **109**
for thoughts on how to say I love God **124**
for Thanksgiving Day **166**
in celebration of God's power **196**

PRAYERS OF WORSHIP AND PRAISE
because I am living and breathing **4**
to celebrate God, who is holy **26**
a song for worshiping together **31**
to celebrate God's creation **48**
to celebrate God's goodness **134**
to celebrate the risen Christ **156**
in celebration of God's power **196**

MORNING PRAYERS
about mornings **12**
on things to think about today **35**
about listening to my Shepherd **52**
thoughts on how to say I love God **124**
a promise to spend time with God **181**

EVENING PRAYERS
about wanting to be good **16**
when I am afraid in the dark **68**
after something grand has happened **88**
about forgiveness for selfish prayers **162**

TABLE PRAYERS
for God's gifts of food **22**
for God's invention of tasty foods **109**
for Thanksgiving Day **166**

PRAYERS FOR FORGIVENESS
when I hurt others and make God sad **1**
when I forget to talk to God **19**
when I am angry and blow my top **72**
when I have disobeyed **139**
because I often don't pray as I ought **162**

203

PRAYERS FOR OTHERS

PRAYERS FOR GOD'S HELP

"TOGETHER" PRAYERS

PRAYERS FOR SPECIAL OCCASIONS

THE PERFECT PRAYER

Scripture Index

The 44 Sounds of the English Language

VOWEL SOUNDS

Short Vowel Sounds

1. a (cap)
2. e (bed)
3. i (fish)
4. o (pop)
5. u (cup, son)

Long Vowel Sounds

6. a (lake, pray, main, they, yea)
7. e (feet, eat, people, believe, baby)
8. i (kite, night, cry, buy)
9. o (go, home, low)
10. u [yoo] (mule, few)

More Vowel Sounds

11. uh (asleep, Jonathan, Israel, Goliath)
12. air (care, hair, scary, bear, their, very)
13. er (her, bird, worry, curl)
14. ah (father, jar)
15. aw (ball, saw, talk, cross)
16. oi (oil, boy)
17. ou (house, down)
18. oo (moon, to, new, June)
19. oo (book, bush, could)

CONSONANT SOUNDS

Single Letters

20. b (boat)
21. d (dog)
22. f (fox, alphabet, laugh)
23. g (gate)

24. h (hat)
25. j (Jericho, giant, page, judge)
26. k (cat, king, back)
27. l (lamp)
28. m (mop)
29. n (nest)
30. p (pig)
31. r (rat, write)
32. s (sun, face)
33. t (ten)
34. v (vase)
35. w (water)
36. y (yarn)
37. z (zebra, nose)

Digraphs
(Two letters that make one new sound)
38. ch (chair, lunch)
39. sh (shark, fish, nation)
40. zh (treasure, vision)
41. th (thank, teeth)
42. th (the, together)
43. hw (wheel)
44. ng (king)

These are the sounds of our language that are addressed by all systems of phonetic instruction. Practice in recognizing letter combinations that stand for these sounds will empower young learners in their quest to become good readers.

Blends and clusters: Several letters can be combined to form a variety of beginning and ending consonant blends and clusters. However, these combinations create no new sounds. There is simply a blend of two or three of the forty-four sounds.

Silent letters: Some words contain letters that are silent. Of course, silent letters can't create a new sound either! So the total number of sounds stays at forty-four.

JOY MACKENZIE, the oldest daughter of a preacher-dad and a teacher-mom, grew up in a loving home where supper was served with Scripture and Shakespeare. As a result, she developed a love for God and people as well as a lifelong romance with words and teaching.

"Perhaps," says Joy, "though I grew older, I never really grew up, for I am still as delighted and intrigued with the Bible stories of my childhood as when they were first read to me. In those early years I also discovered that conversation with God, my heavenly Daddy, was possible. As an adult, I still cherish that perspective of Father-daughter communication; only now I understand what a privilege it is!"

Joy's continuing enthusiasm for kid stuff is evident in her professional life, which has included teaching every elementary and high school grade (working with both gifted and academically challenged students), six years of teaching at the college level, touring nationwide as an educational consultant, serving twenty years as vice president of an educational publishing company, and authoring more than fifty books. Her published works include many resources for teachers and dozens of religious books and recordings for children and their families.

As chairman of the English department at Nashville's Christ Presbyterian Academy, this lover of literature and life divides her time between teaching, writing, speaking, consulting, and being "Mom" to two grown daughters.

JILL NEWTON was born in Newcastle, England (in the northeast part of the country). She grew up in Lincoln, where she learned to ride and fall off bicycles and horses and did a lot of other fun stuff when she was at school.

Jill studied art at Lincoln Art College and illustration at Cambridge College of Art. She explains that Cambridge was very cold, so when she finished her studies she moved to London (Hackney), where she stayed for fourteen years. She claims that this is quite an achievement by most people's standards.

A nature lover and friend of animals, Jill now lives in a small village in Somerset with her good horse, Samuel, who has been with her since he gave up racing a number of years ago. Jill says her horse tells her he has no intention of returning. (Jill has told Sam not to worry. She doesn't think he is going to be asked back.) Benjamin, the sheep puppy, has come to stay too. He and Jill go out exploring together.

Jill has been illustrating children's books since she left college. She has also worked in advertising, design, and TV. In addition, she had a brief escapade as a bicycle courier, delivering a variety of packages to their destination.

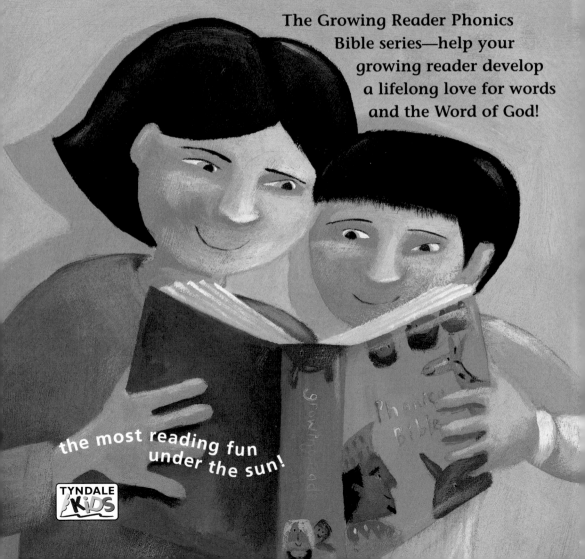

Phonics-based ❂ Fun to read ❂ Biblically faithful

The Growing Reader Phonics Bible is packed full of Bible stories that kids and parents alike will love to read again and again. . . . A red letter highlights the featured sound in every story so kids can see how letters make sounds and sounds make words.

Listening Edition
ISBN 0-8423-8624-6

Kids will love to listen along as real kids read their favorite Bible stories to them. Early readers can follow along and increase their understanding of the phonics sounds.

The Growing Reader Phonics Bible series—help your growing reader develop a lifelong love for words and the Word of God!

the most reading fun under the sun!

TYNDALE KIDS